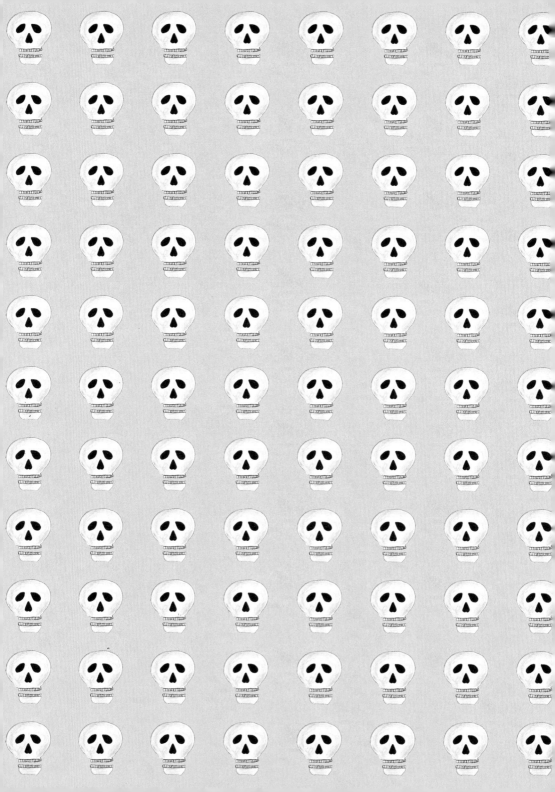

EVERYBODY DIES

To Alex, Ken Tanaka

Loves you

Everybody Dies

A Children's Book

for Grown-Ups

by Ken Tanaka

with David Ury

HARPER DESIGN
An Imprint of HarperCollins Publishers

A Maximum Pleasant Book

EVERYBODY DIES: A CHILDREN'S BOOK FOR GROWN-UPS

Harper Collins books may be purchased for educational, business, or sales promotional use. For information, please e-mail the Special Markets Department at SPsales@harpercollins.com.

Published in 2014 by:
Harper Design
An Imprint of HarperCollins Publishers
10 East 53rd Street
New York, NY 10022
Tel (212) 207-7000
harperdesign@harpercollins.com
www.harpercollins.com

Distributed throughout the world by:
HarperCollins Publishers
10 East 53rd Street
New York, NY 10022
Library of Congress Control Number: 2013952640
ISBN: 978-0-06-232964-6
Printed in China, 2014

Illustration editing by Cam Floyd

Dedicated to Lisa Nguyen,
who should have been
the exception

"He who pretends
to look on death
without fear,
lies."

— Jean-Jacques Rousseau, Julie, or the New Heloise

"We die only once
and
for such a long time."
—Molière

It's an introduction

Oh hello, I'm not sure if we have met before. I'm Ken Tanaka. How are you? I am fine. Thank you very much. I'm glad to know that you are reading my picture book. It is my hope that the many happy animals and people in this book will help you understand the inevitable fate that awaits us all. Sometimes people ask me why I wrote a "children's book for grown-ups." People seem to think that children need to be sheltered from the idea of death, but most children I have met are not afraid of death, or of this book. It is the grown-ups who shake in fear when they read the words Everybody Dies. Grown-ups are afraid of death. Grown-ups know that it is coming, and it can't be stopped.

When we are truly overcome with fear, we are still children on the inside, no matter our age. We still want our mommies. Sometimes grown-ups need to be treated like children for their own good. And so here it is, "Everybody Dies: A Children's Book for Grown-ups."

Although meant for adults, this book may be most effective when read aloud to frightened parents by their children.

Ken Tanaka

EVERY Living Thing Must Someday Die.

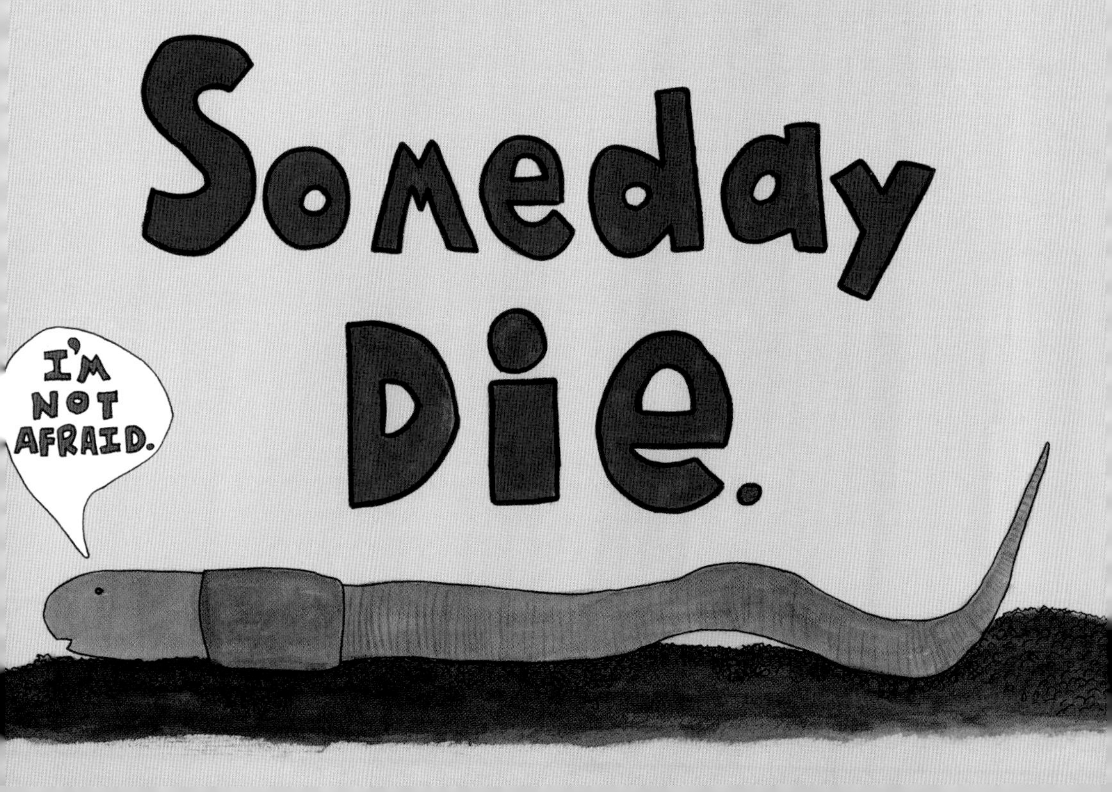

CUTE ANIMALS DIE

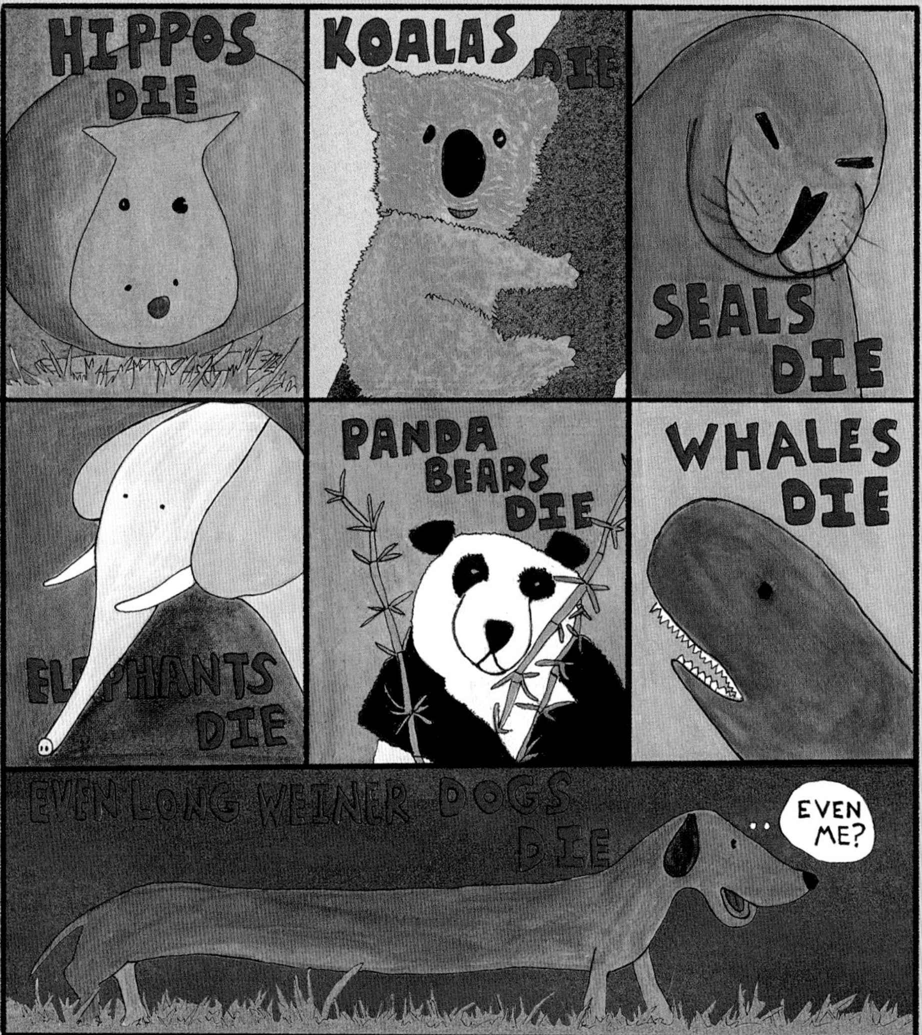

HIPPOS DIE
KOALAS DIE
SEALS DIE
ELEPHANTS DIE
PANDA BEARS DIE
WHALES DIE
EVEN LONG WEINER DOGS DIE
EVEN ME?

AND SO DO SCARY ONES.

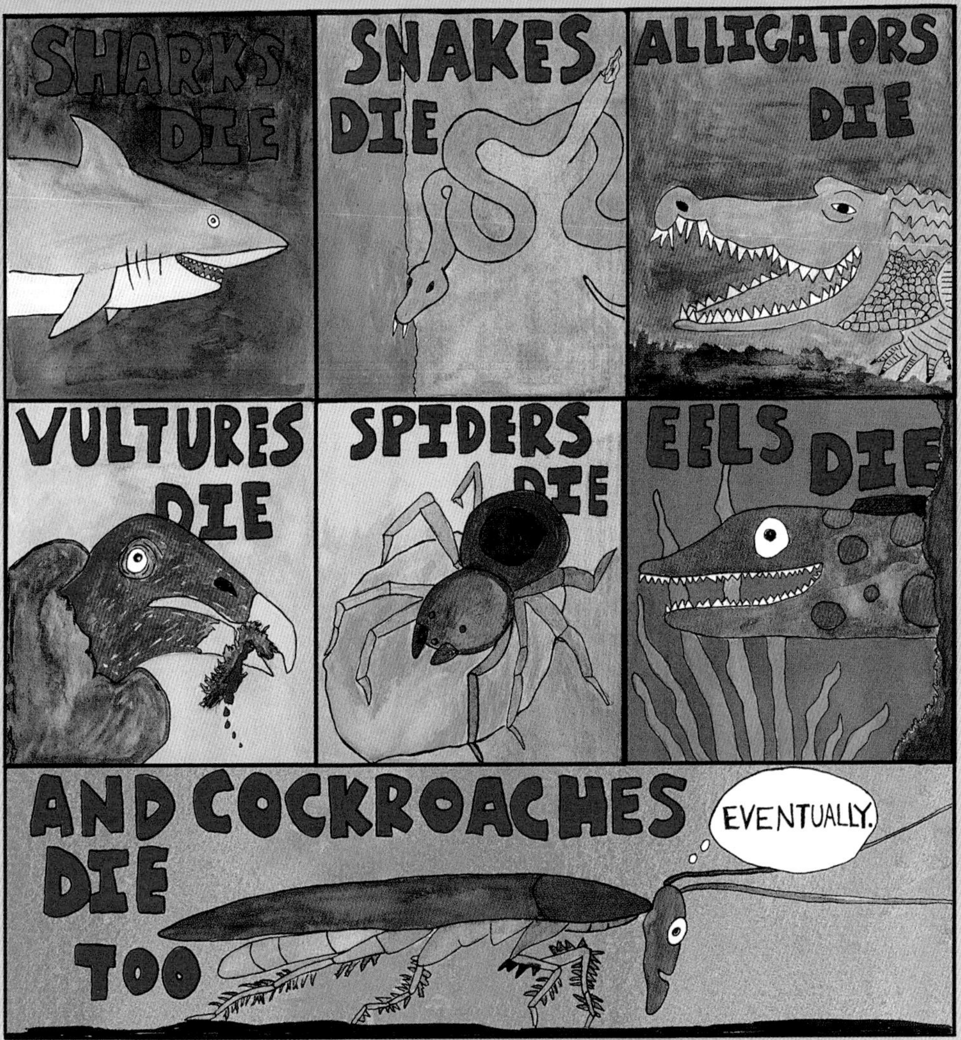
SHARKS DIE
SNAKES DIE
ALLIGATORS DIE
VULTURES DIE
SPIDERS DIE
EELS DIE
AND COCKROACHES DIE TOO
EVENTUALLY.

WHEN

GOLDFISH

DIE

THEY FLOAT TO THE

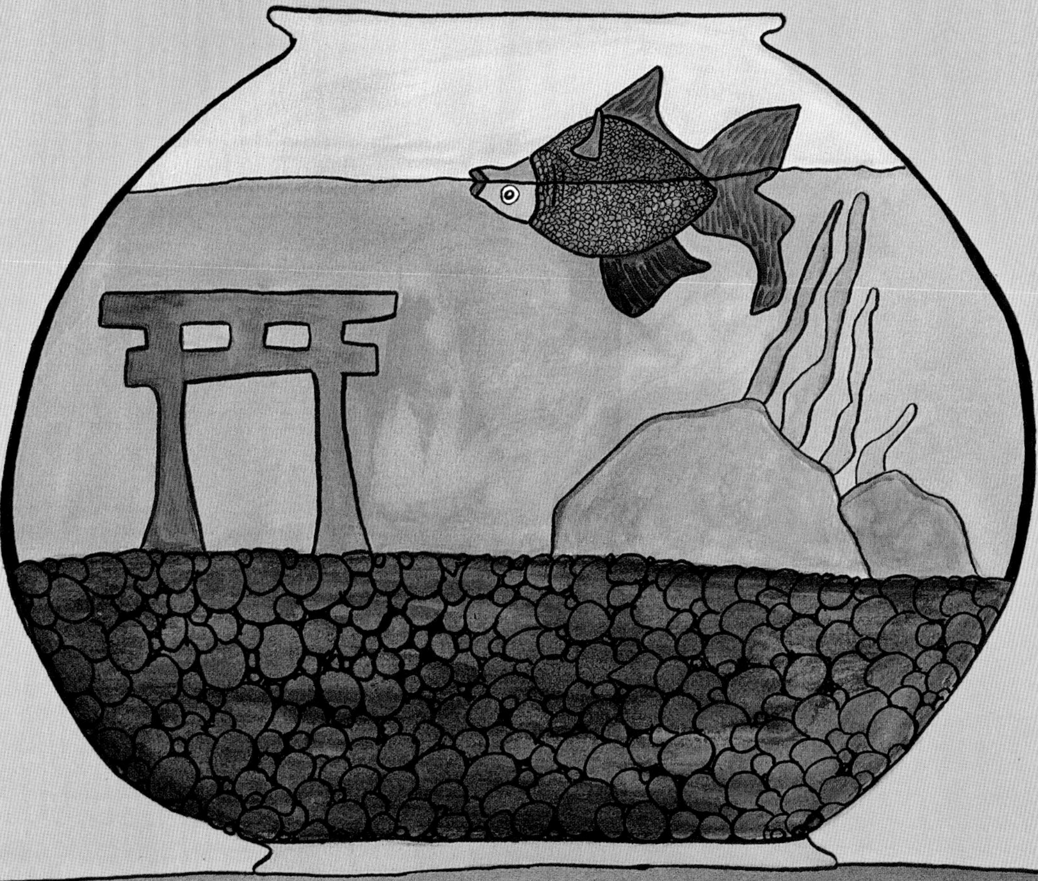

TOP OF THE TANK.

HONEY

BEES

DIE

RIGHT AFTER

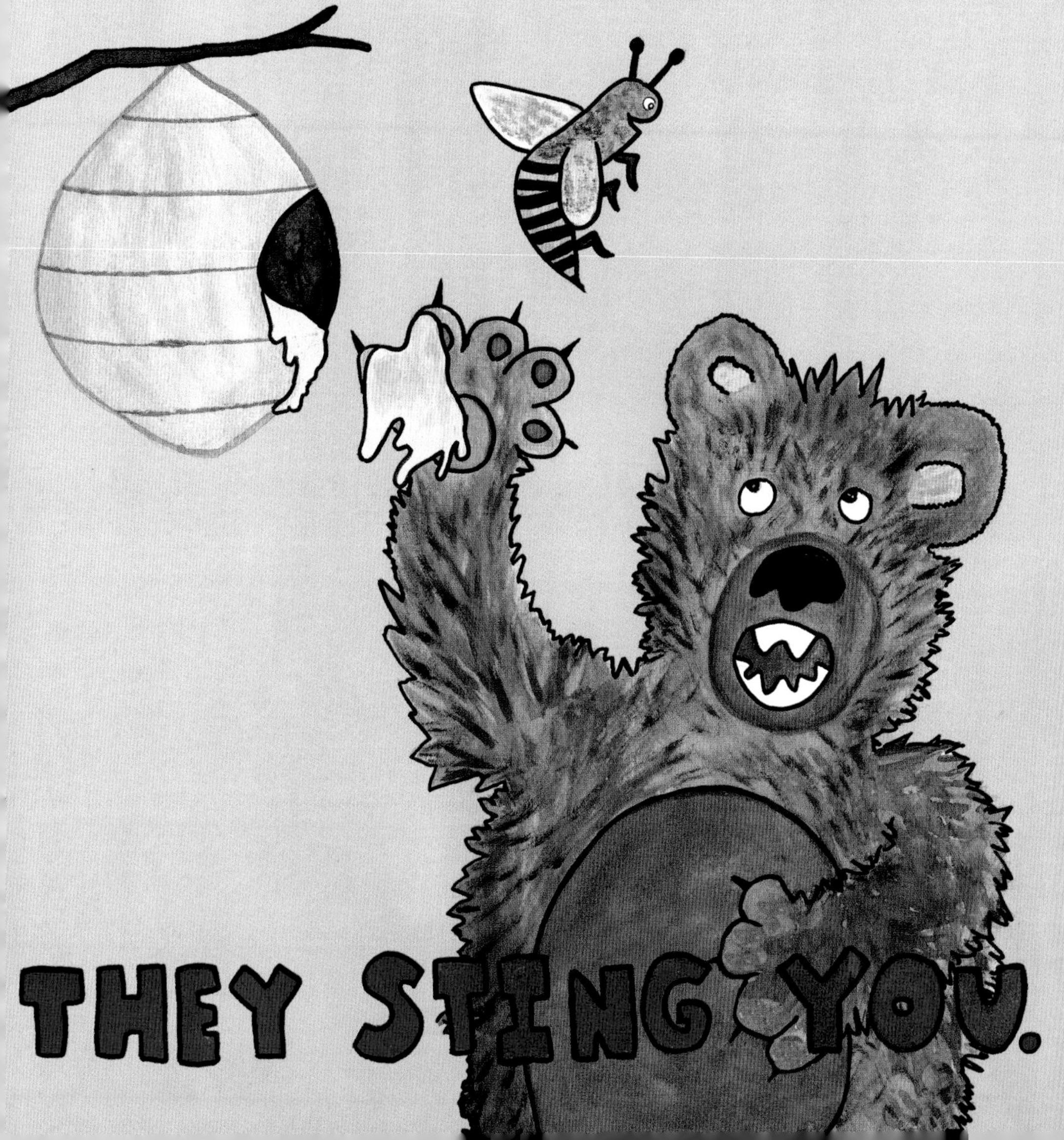

THEY STING YOU.

Some Animals Live for a Very Long Time.

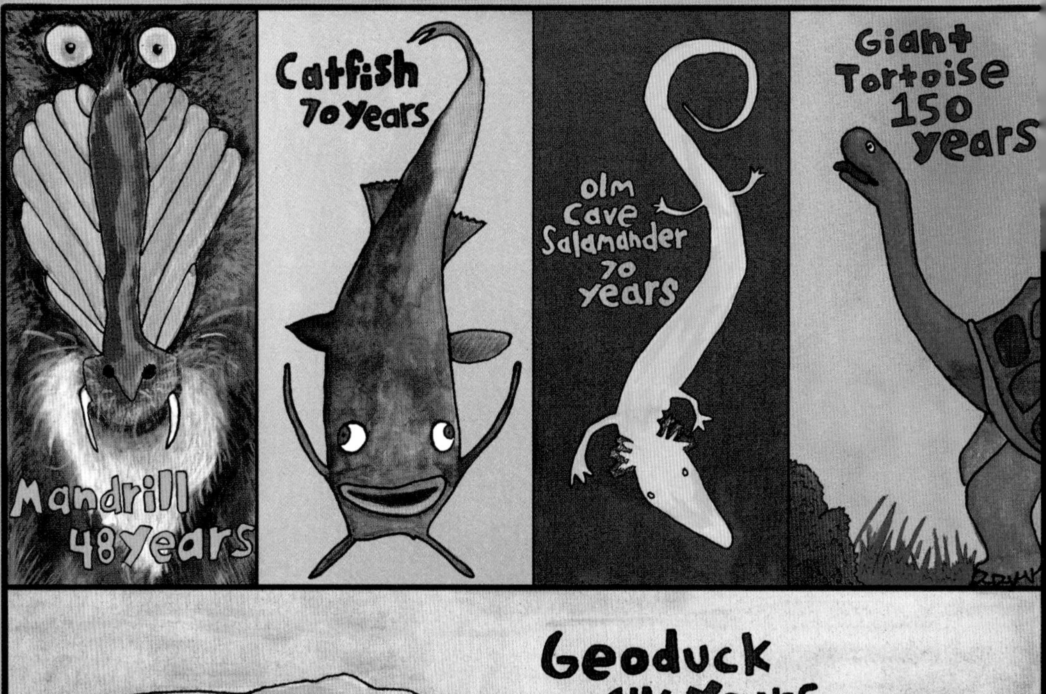
Mandrill
48 years
Catfish
70 years
olm
Cave
Saldmander
70
years
Giant
Tortoise
150
years
Geoduck
146 Years

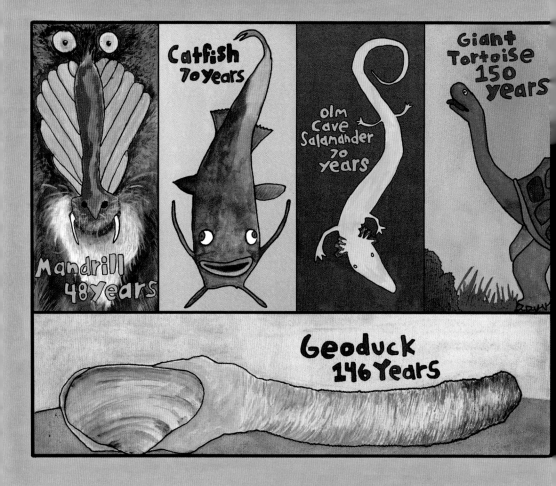

Others Die Right Away.

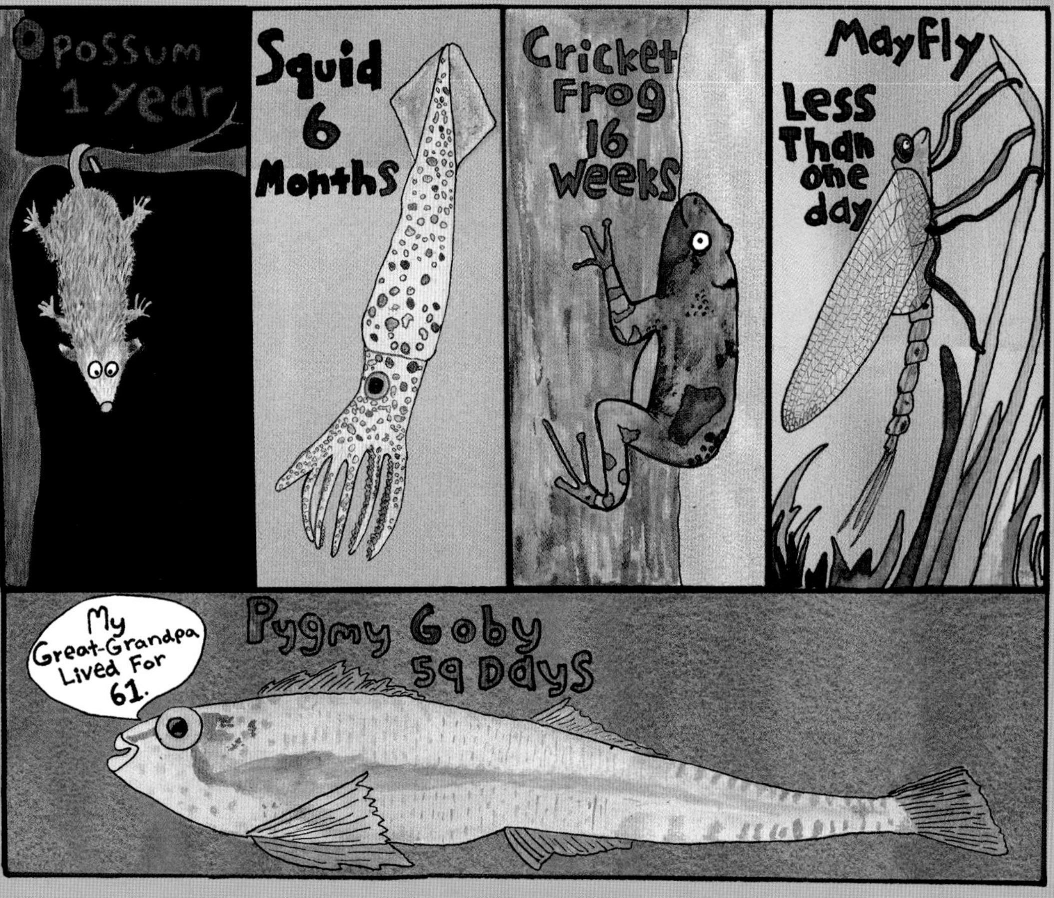
Opossum 1 year
Squid 6 Months
Cricket Frog 16 Weeks
Mayfly Less Than one day
Pygmy Goby 59 Days
My Great-Grandpa Lived For 61.

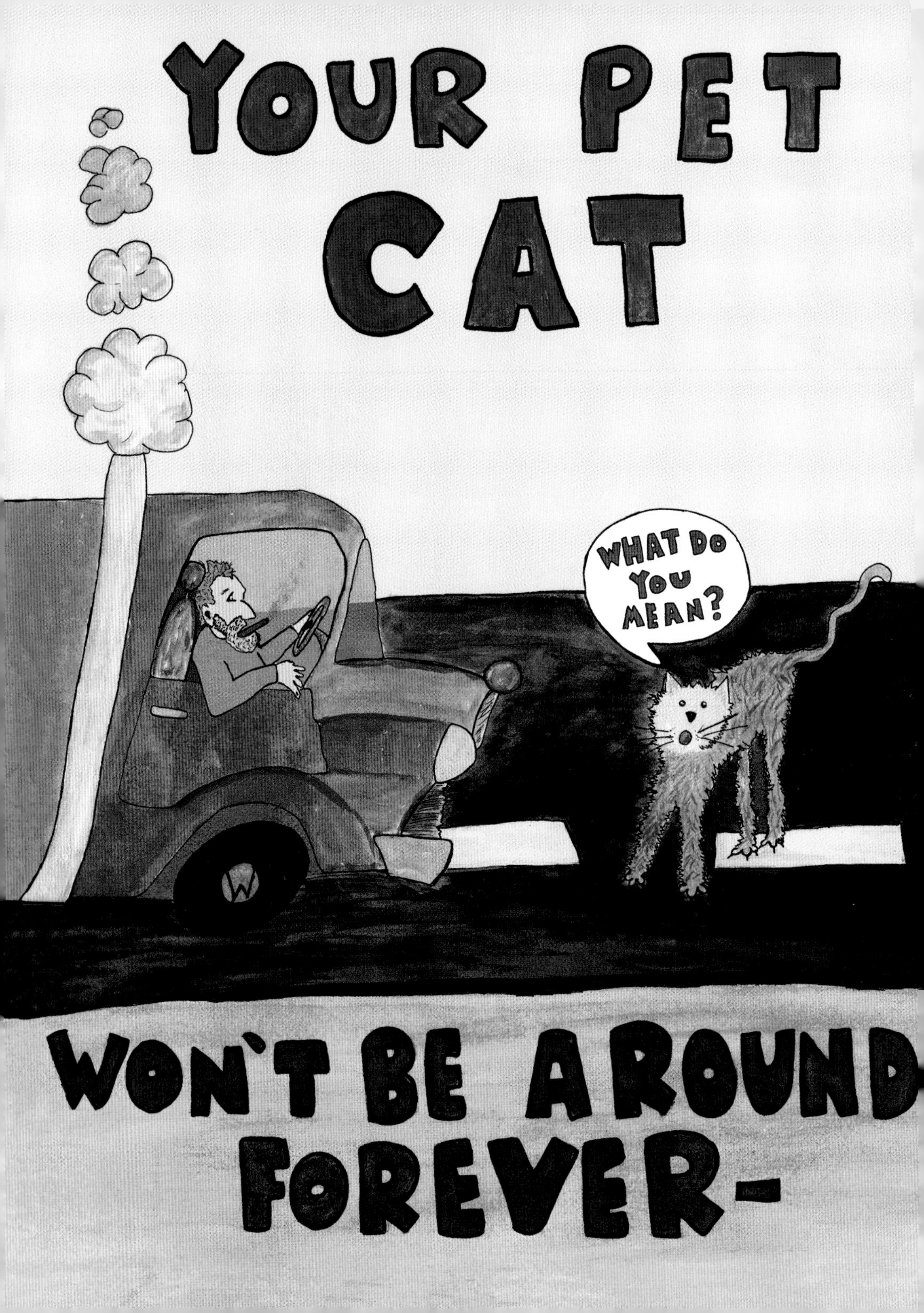
YOUR PET CAT
WHAT DO YOU MEAN?
WON'T BE AROUND FOREVER-

NEITHER WILL MOMMY AND DADDY.

SOME PEOPLE TRY TO AVOID DEATH,

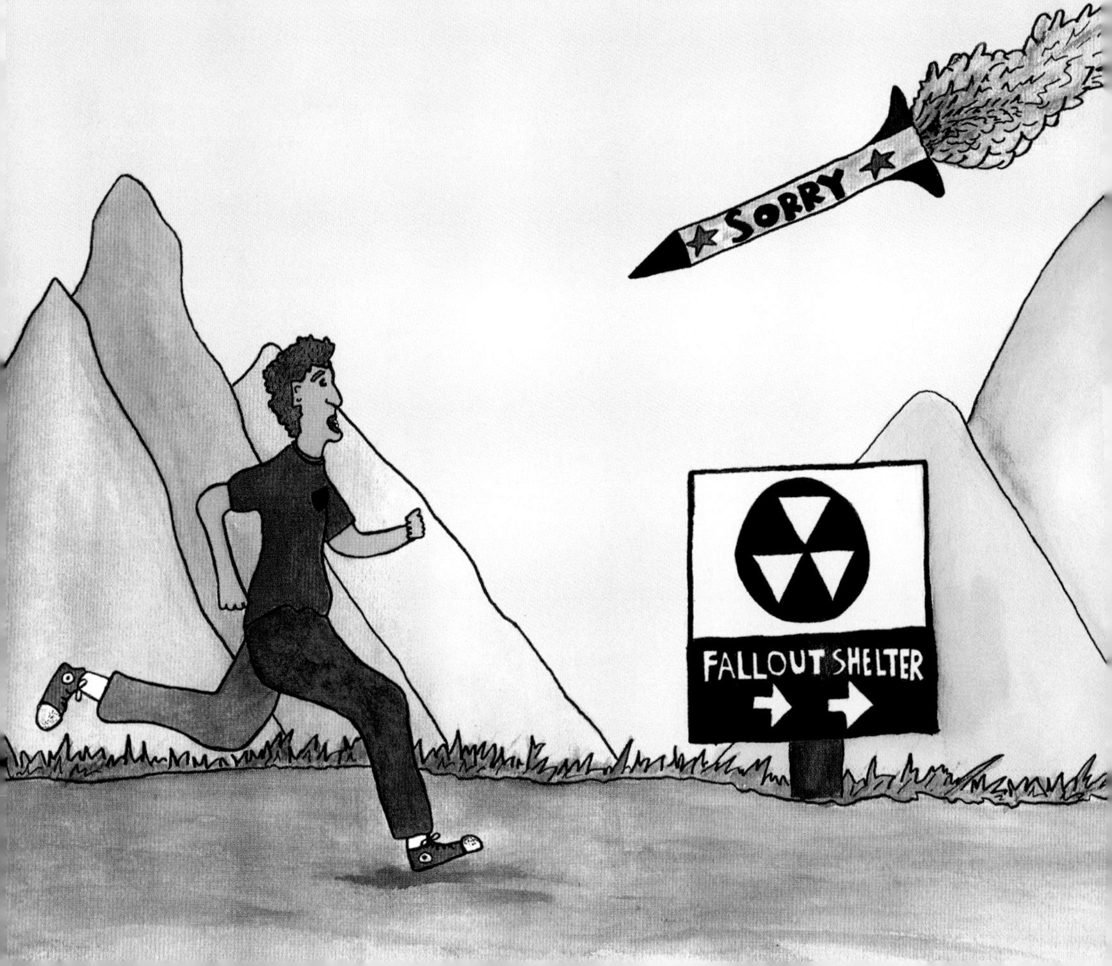
SORRY
FALLOUT SHELTER

OTHERS TRY TO TEMPT IT,

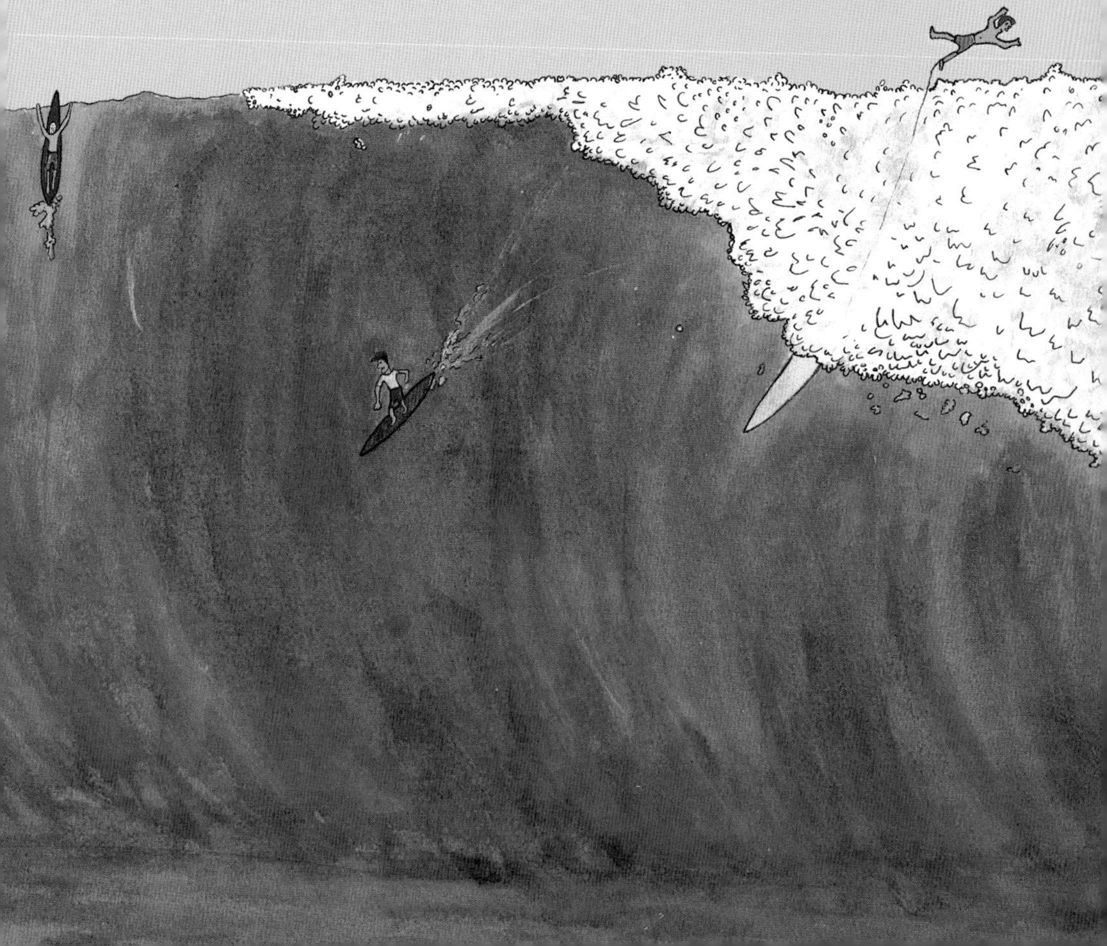

AND OTHERS JUST CAN'T WAIT FOR DEATH.

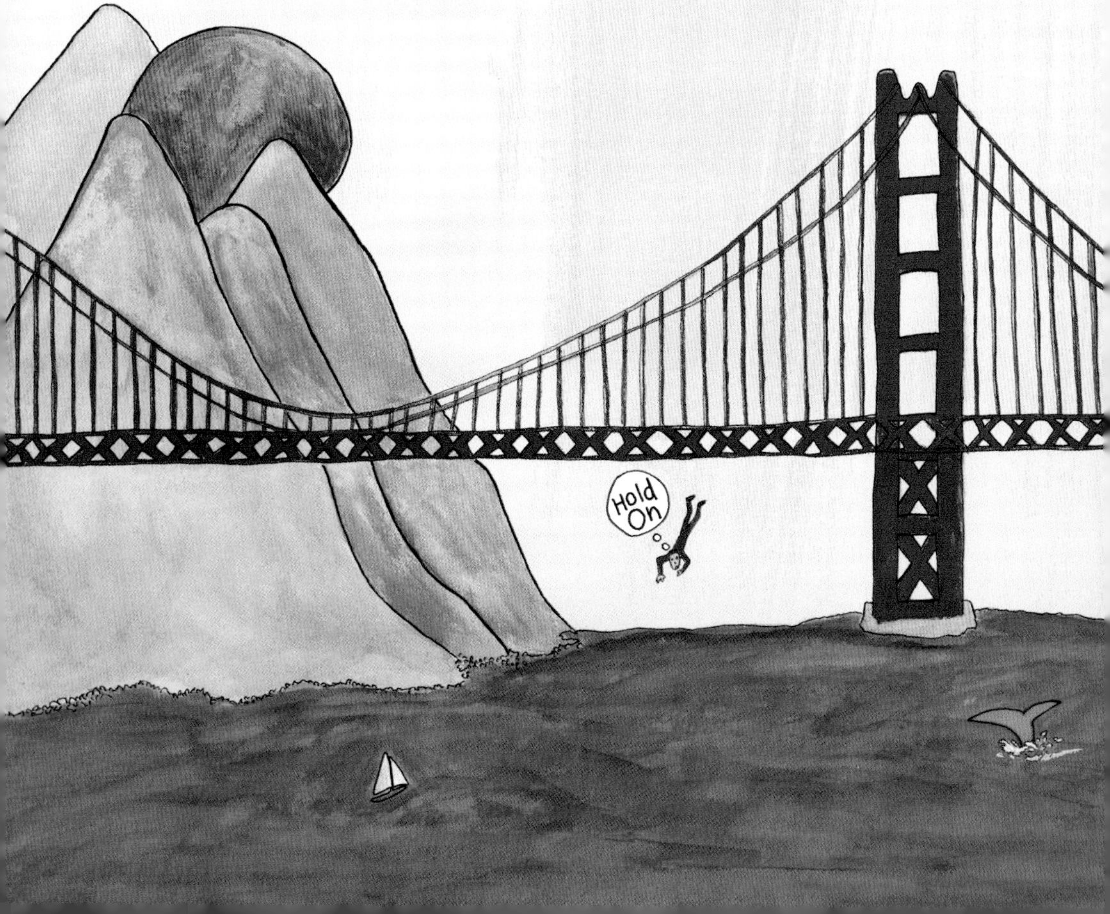
Hold On

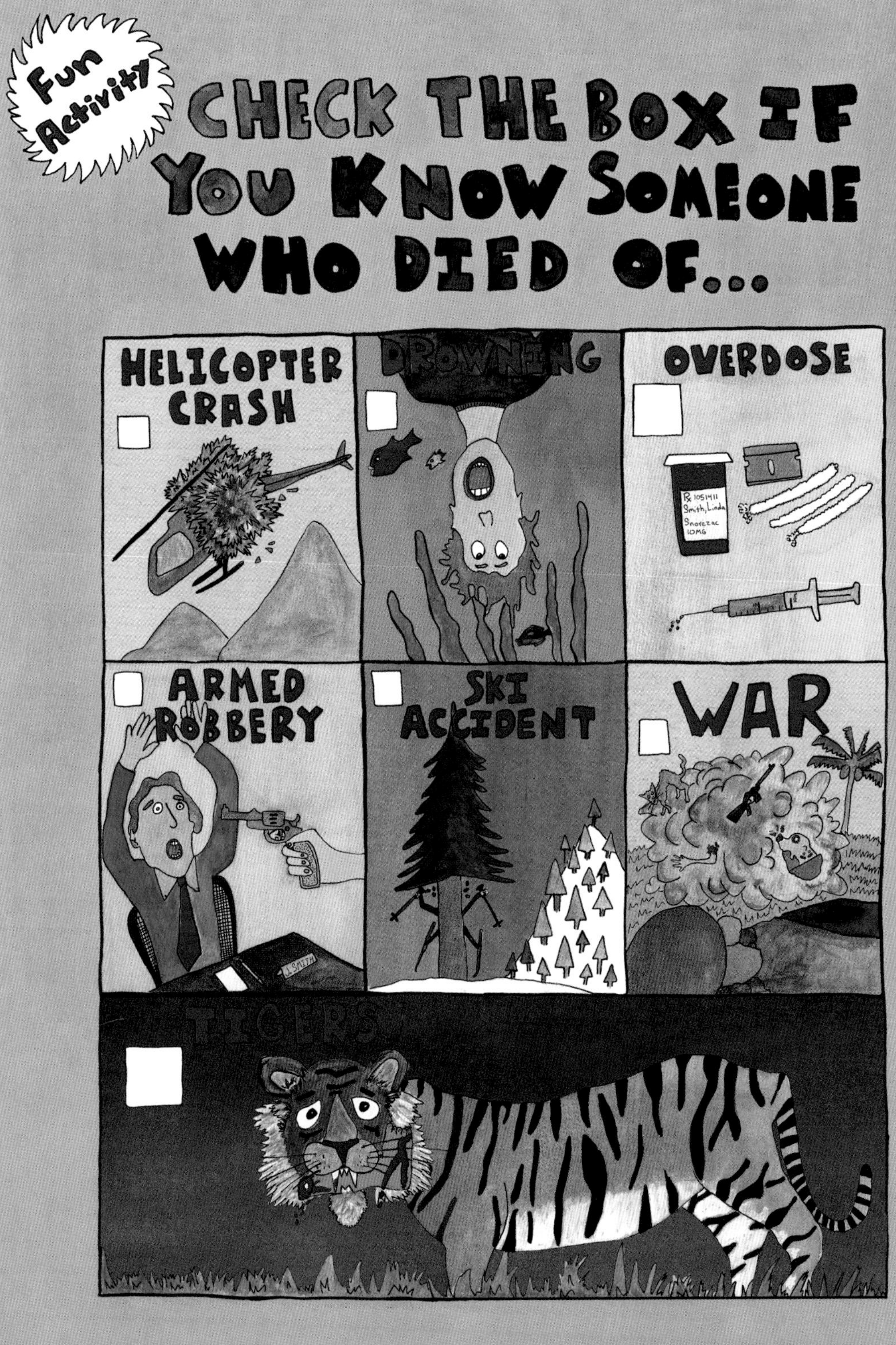
Fun Activity
CHECK THE BOX IF YOU KNOW SOMEONE WHO DIED OF...
HELICOPTER CRASH
DROWNING
OVERDOSE
Rx 1051411
Smith, Linda
Snorezac
10MG
ARMED ROBBERY
J.SMITH
SKI ACCIDENT
WAR
TIGERS

NO BODY LIKES TO THINK ABOUT DEATH,

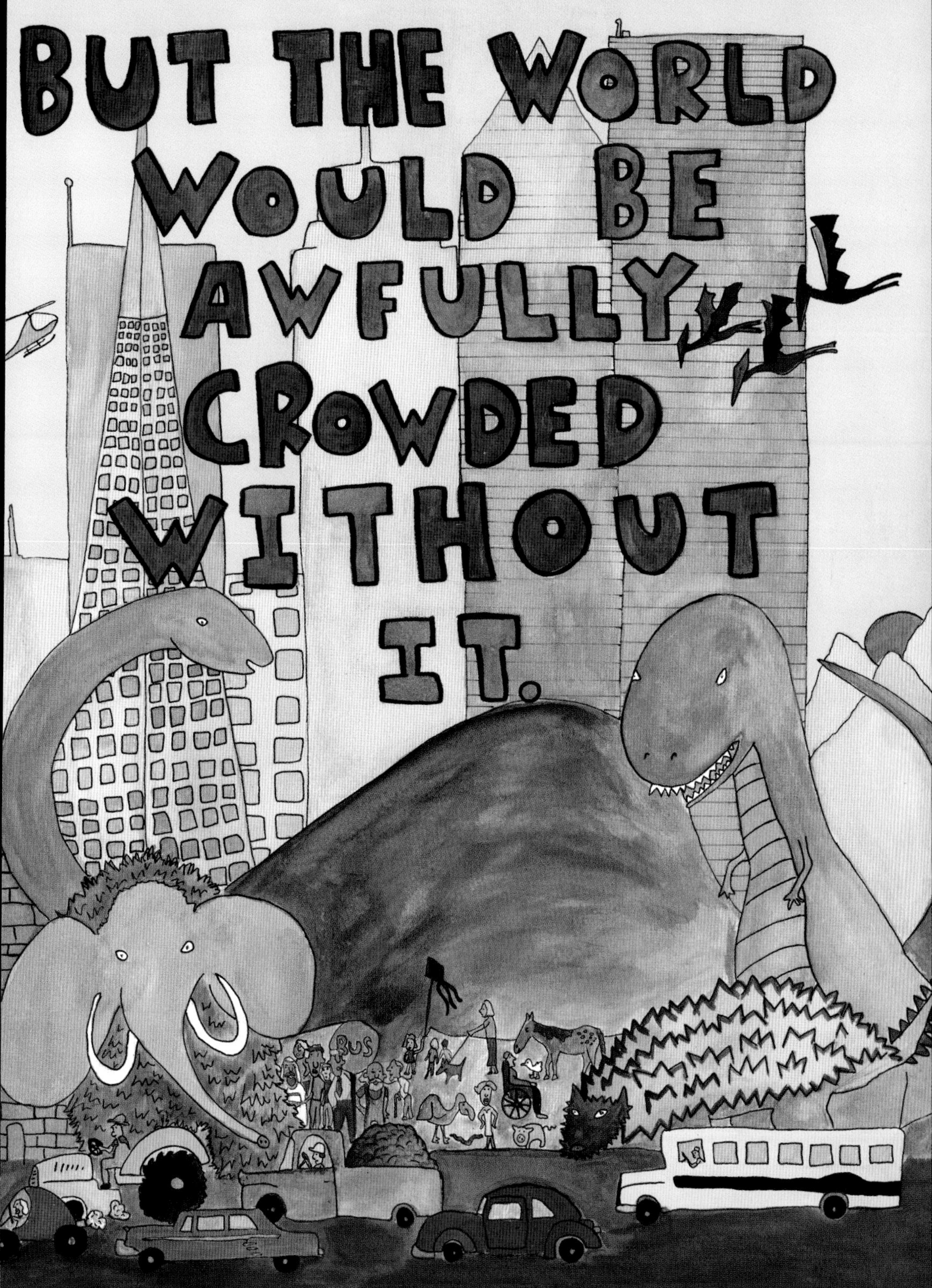
BUT THE WORLD WOULD BE AWFULLY CROWDED WITHOUT IT.
BUS

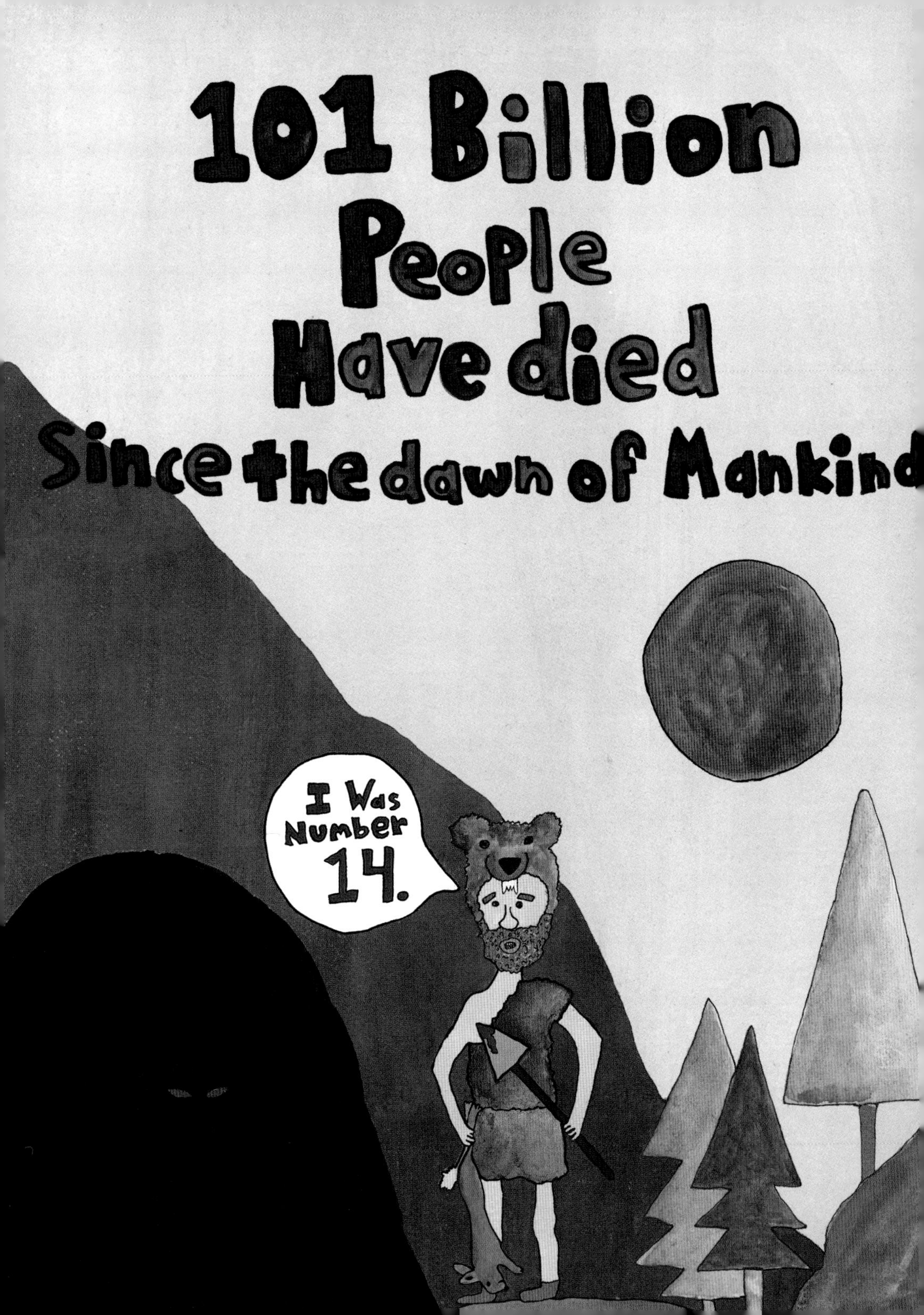
101 Billion People Have died Since the dawn of Mankind
I Was Number 14.

Fun Activity

Match the Corpse to the Cause of Death

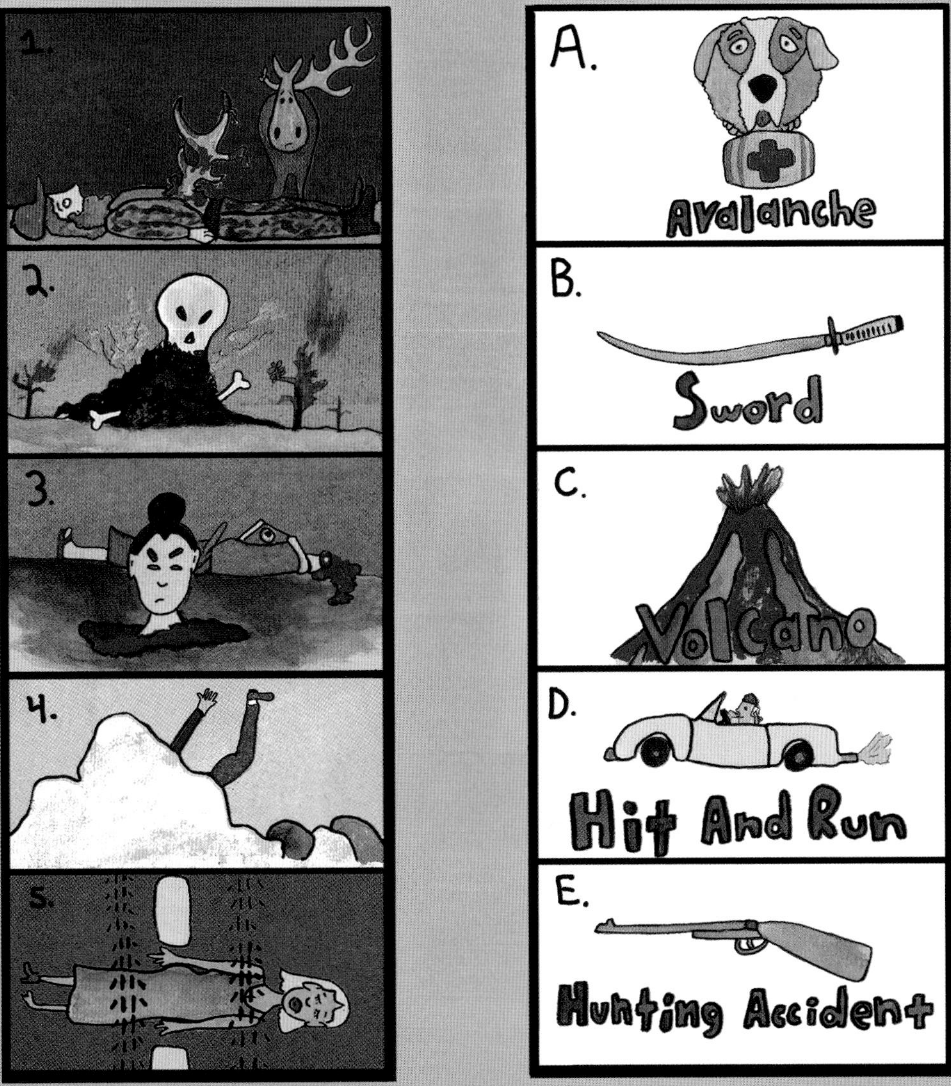

1.
2.
3.
4.
5.
A.
Avalanche
B.
Sword
C.
Volcano
D.
Hit And Run
E.
Hunting Accident

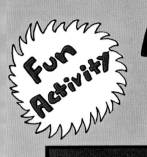

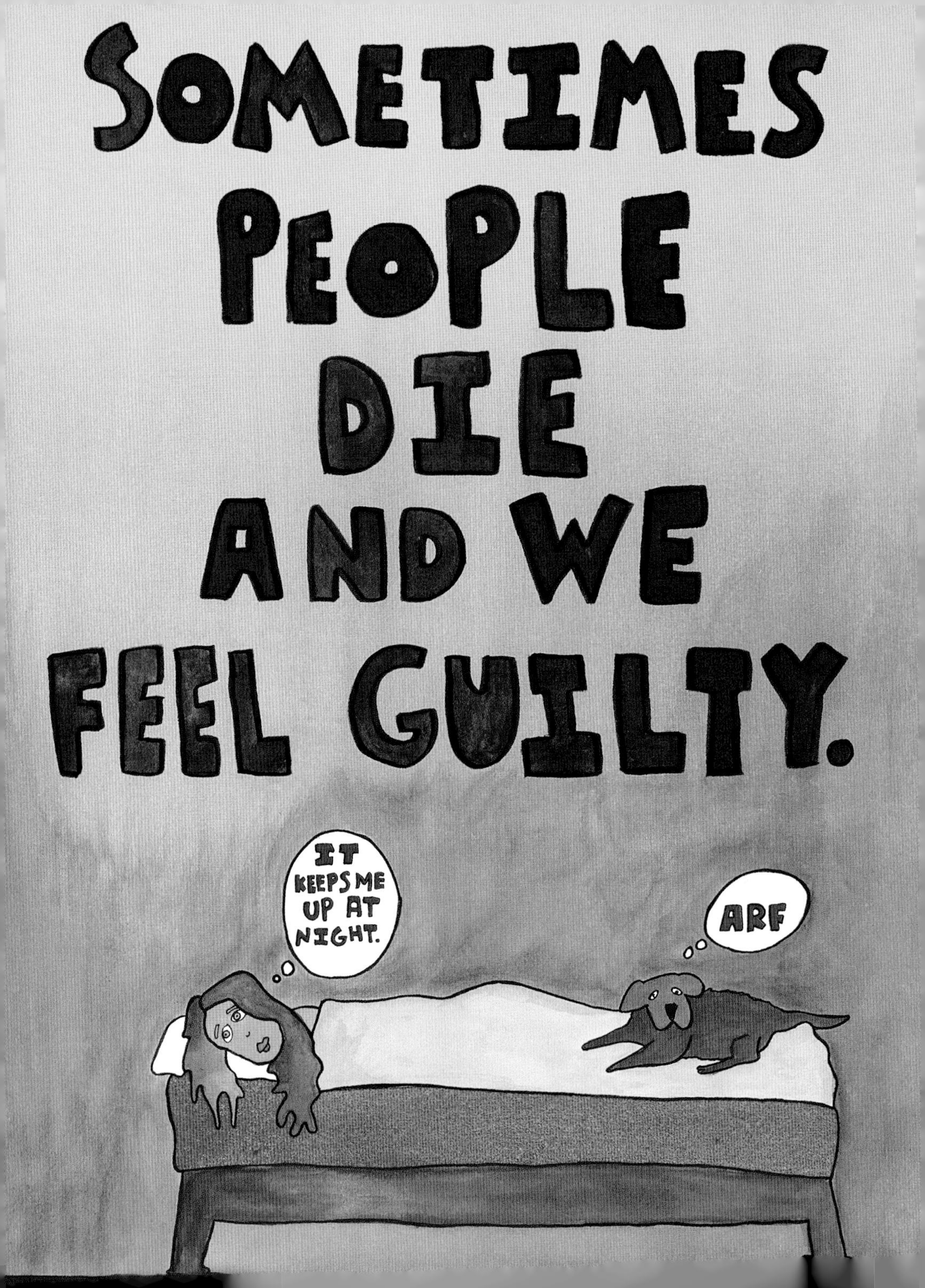
SOMETIMES PEOPLE DIE AND WE FEEL GUILTY.
IT KEEPS ME UP AT NIGHT.
ARF

DID YOU TELL GRANDMA YOU LOVED HER BEFORE HER STROKE?

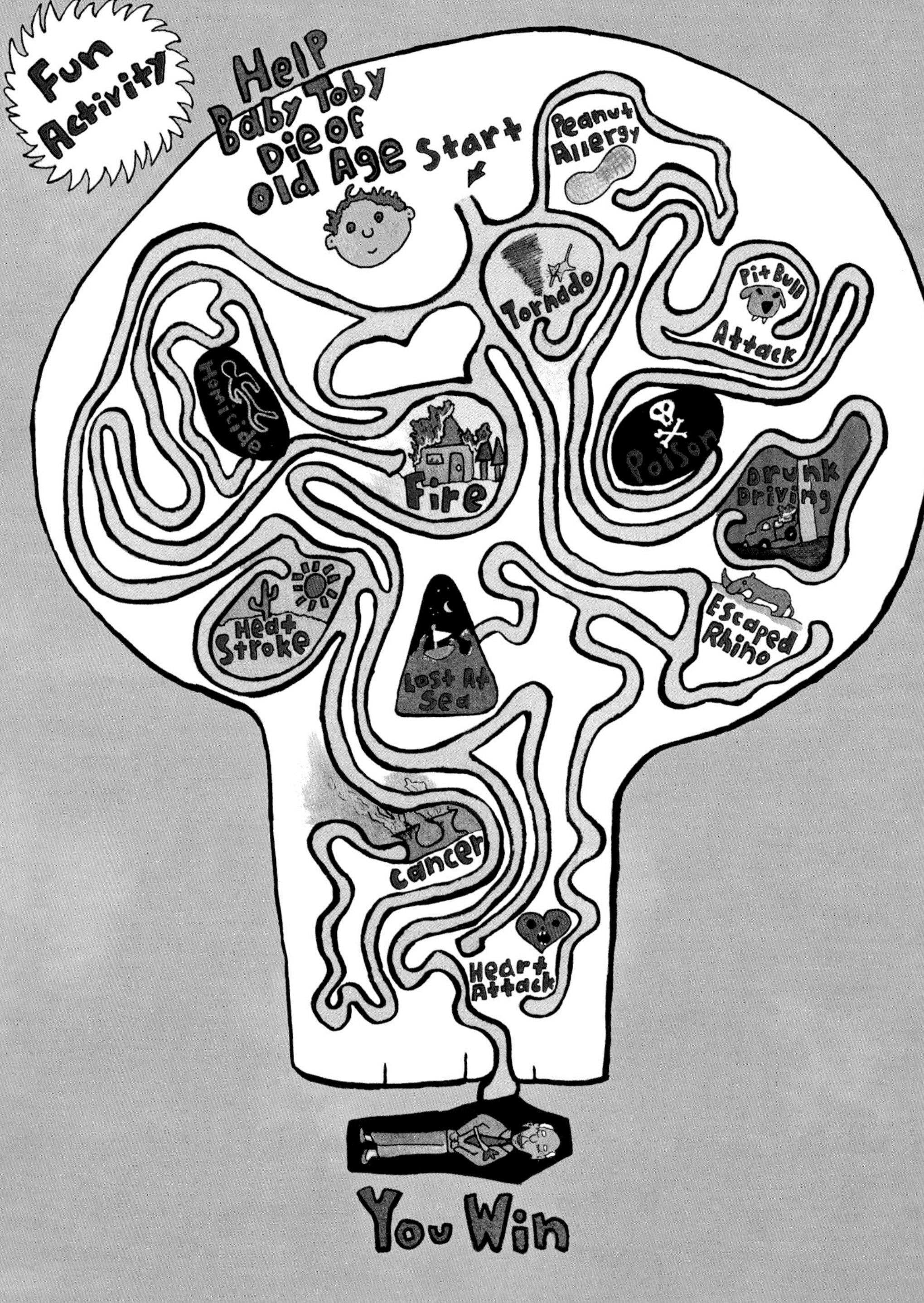
Fun Activity
Help Baby Toby Die of Old Age
Start
Peanut Allergy
Tornado
Pit Bull Attack
Homicide
Fire
Poison
Drunk Driving
Escaped Rhino
Heat Stroke
Lost At Sea
Cancer
Heart Attack
You Win

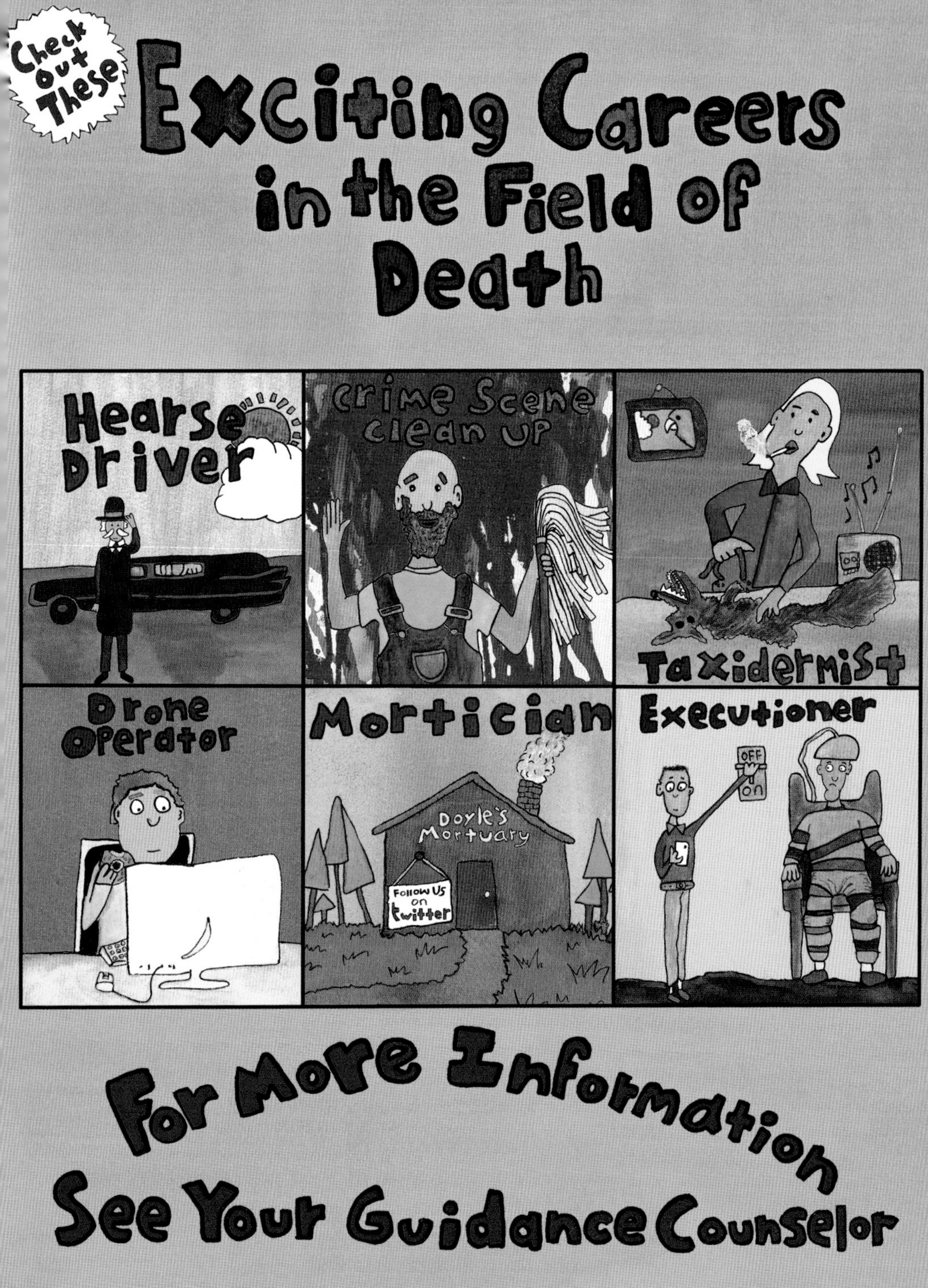
Check out These
Exciting Careers in the Field of Death
Hearse Driver
crime Scene clean up
Taxidermist
Drone Operator
Mortician
Doyle's Mortuary
Follow Us on twitter
Executioner
OFF
on
For More Information
See Your Guidance Counselor

157 PEOPLE DIE EVERY 60 SECONDS.

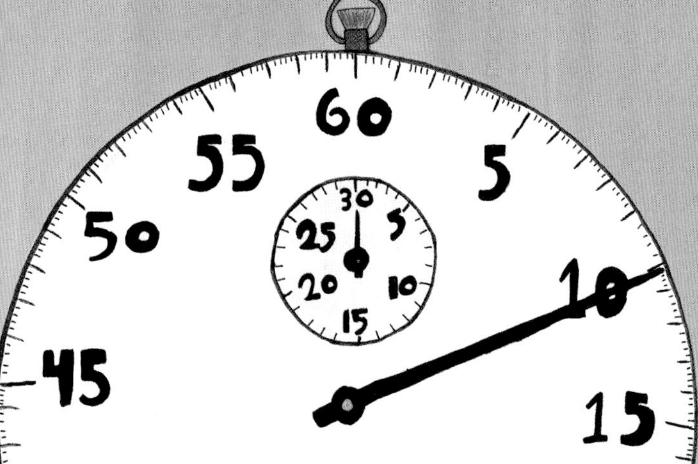
60
5
10
15
20
25
30
35
40
45
50
55
30
5
10
15
20
25
Taraka
1/5 SEC

ARE YOU STILL THERE?

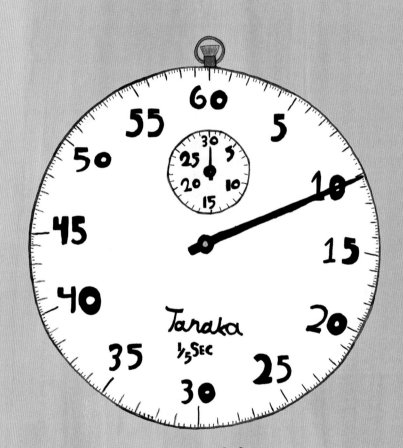

RIGHT NOW YOU ARE FIT AND HEALTHY,

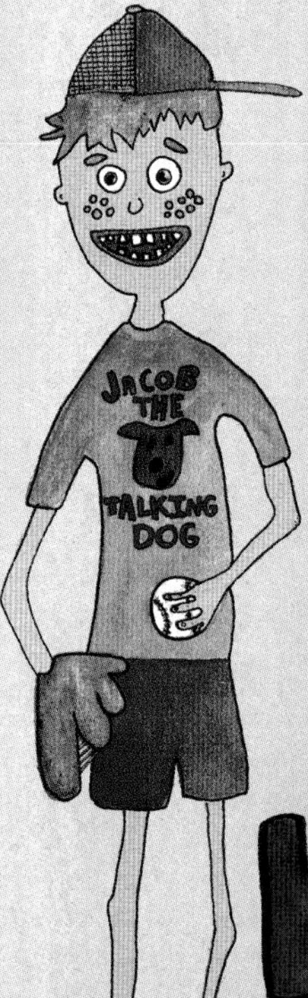
JACOB THE TALKING DOG

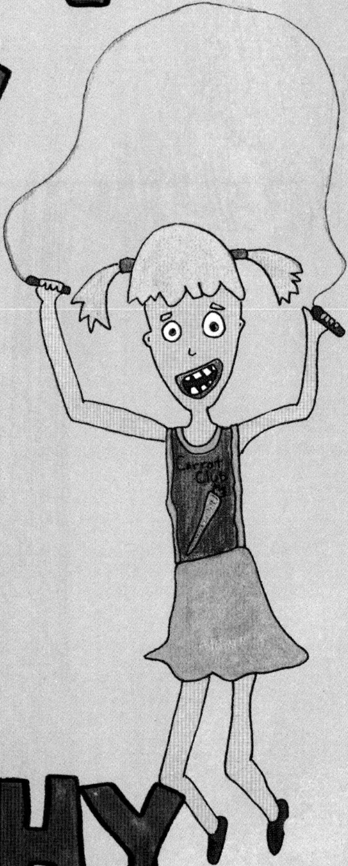
Carrot Club

BUT YOU WON'T ALWAYS BE.

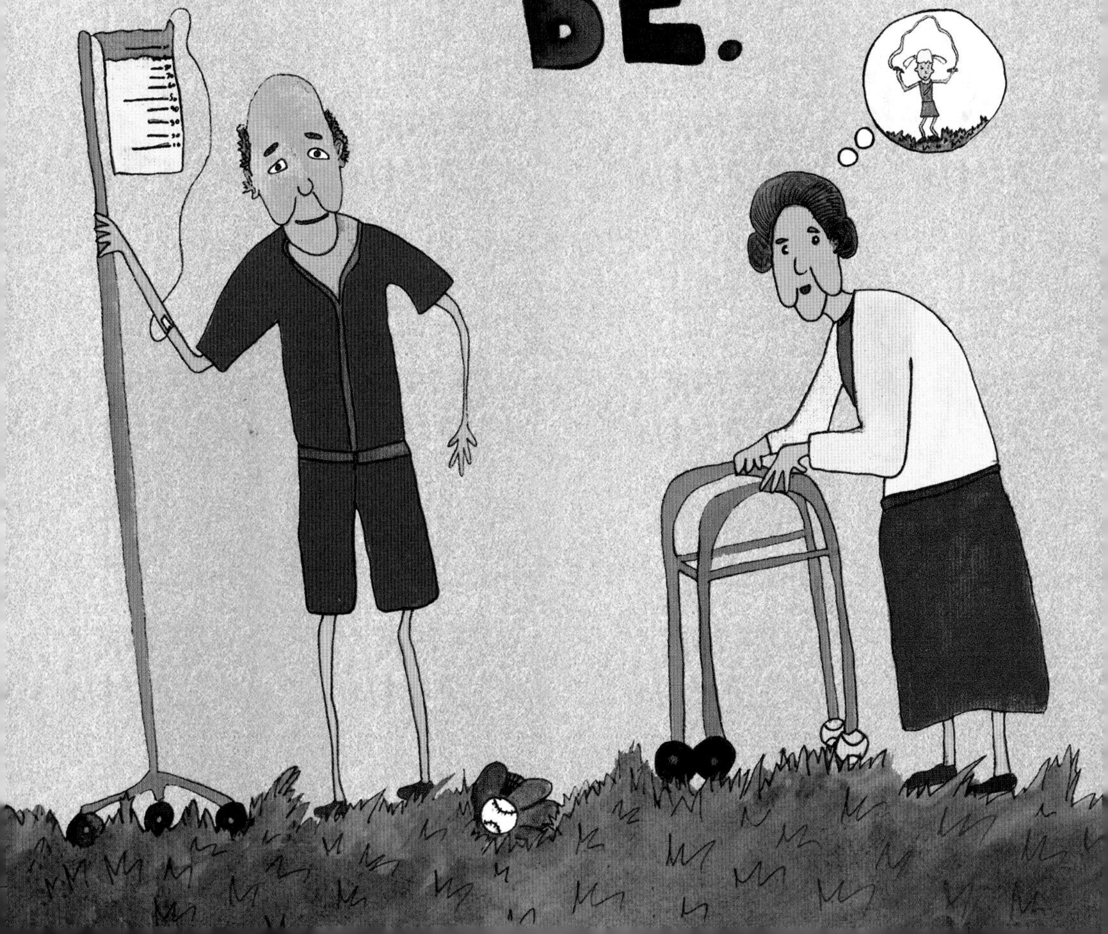

HERE ARE SOME DISEASES THAT COULD BE KILLING YOU RIGHT NOW

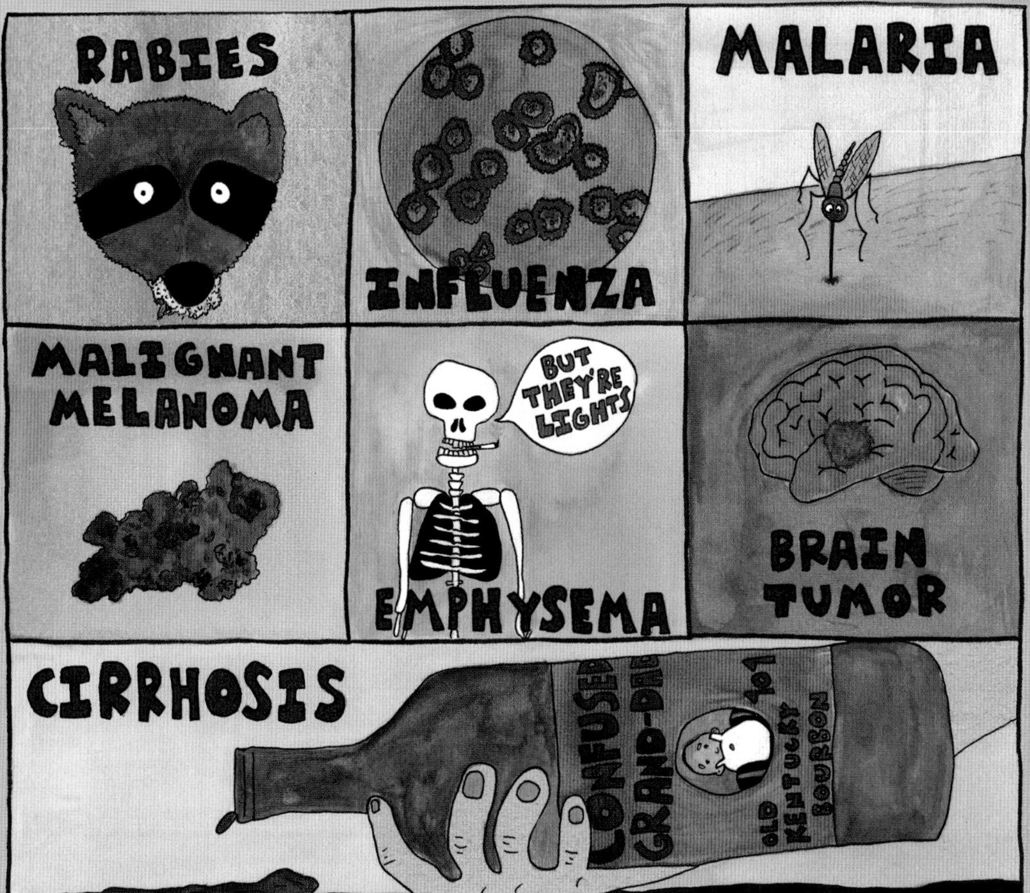

RABIES
INFLUENZA
MALARIA
MALIGNANT MELANOMA
BUT THEY'RE LIGHTS
EMPHYSEMA
BRAIN TUMOR
CIRRHOSIS
CONFUSED GRAND-DAD
OLD KENTUCKY BOURBON

EVERYBODY DIES,

AND SOMEDAY YOU WILL TOO.

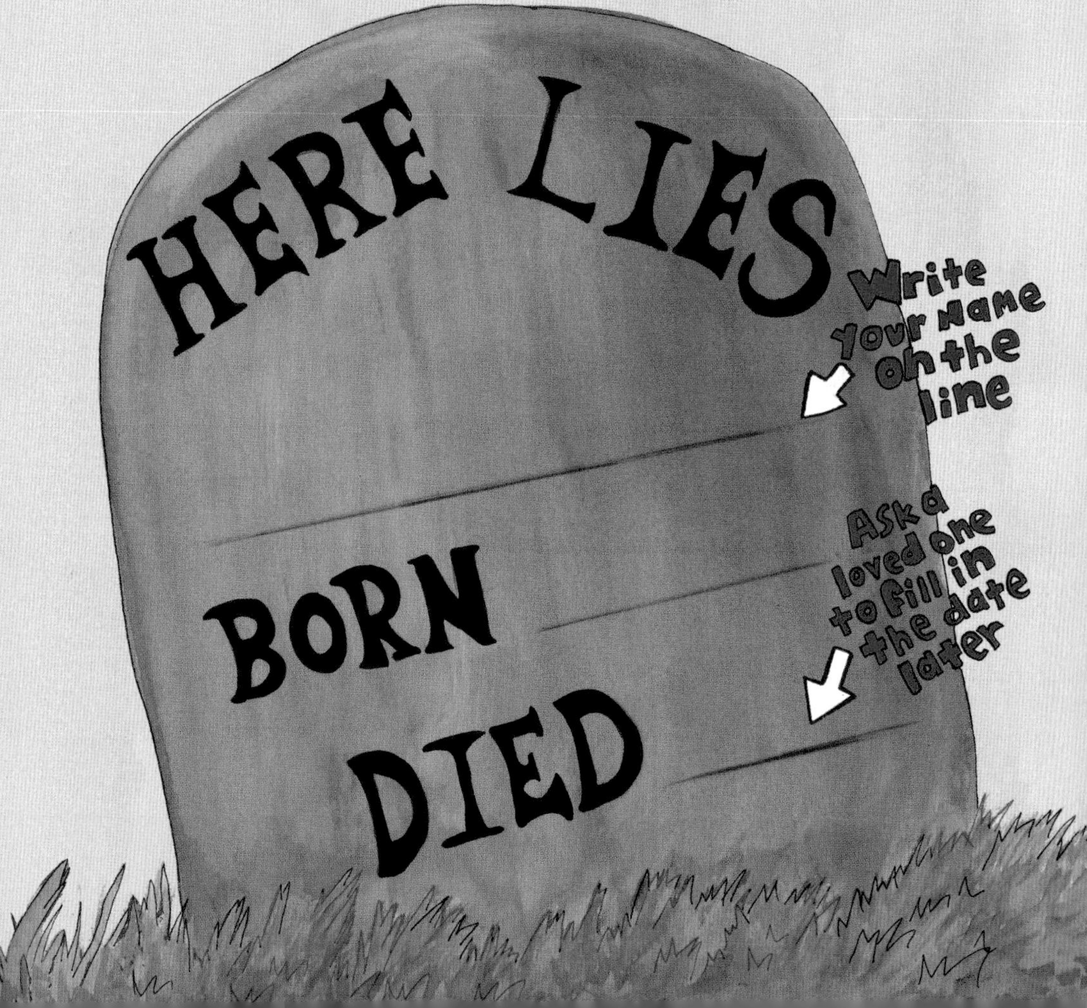
HERE LIES
Write your name on the line
BORN
Ask a loved one to fill in the date later
DIED

Fill out your very own Will*

Last Will And Testament
of _____

I _____, age _____, residing at _____ in
       NAME
_____, being of sound mind, hereby declare
this to be my Last Will and Testament, revoking
all wills and codicils previously made by me.

1. I appoint _____ as my executor to
administer my estate. If _____ is unable or
unwilling to serve as my executor, then I
appoint _____ as my executor, and ask that
he/she be permitted to serve without court supervision
and to act without posting bond.

2. I hereby direct my executor to pay out all
legally enforceable claims against my estate and to
pay all federal and state inheritance taxes, administration
costs, expenses of my last illness and all funerary costs
without the intervention of the court.

3. I hereby bequeath my _____
_____ to _____
I hereby bequeath my _____
_____ to _____
I hereby bequeath my _____
_____ to _____

4. I hereby bequeath the remainder of my residuary estate to the following beneficiaries.

1. ___ % to ____________________
2. ___ % to ____________________
3. ___ % to ____________________

5. If any beneficiary listed above dies within thirty days of my own death, the deceased beneficiary's share shall be divided equally among the beneficiary's surviving children.

Self-Proving Affidavit

We the testator and the witnesses whose names are signed below do hereby declare that this instrument, consisting of these two pages, was the testator's Last Will and Testament, and that the testator, a legal adult appearing to be of sound mind, signed this instrument willingly, as a voluntary act, and was not under duress at the time of signing. Each witness hereby declares that the testator is not a minor. Each witness also declares that he/she signed this instrument at the request of and in the presence of the testator. We the witnesses each declare that each of us is over the age of eighteen and that each of us is and the other appears to be of sound mind. We each declare, under penalty of perjury, that the foregoing is true and correct and that this attestation and declaration are executed on the ____ day of ______ ____ at ____ (time).

Name ________________ Address ____________________

Name ________________ Address ____________________

*This Will is provided for parody and informational purposes, and not for the purpose of providing legal advice. This document is not meant to be used as an actual Last Will and Testament. Laws regarding Last Will and Testaments vary depending on state and territory, and you should always seek your own legal counsel when creating your Last Will and Testament.

THE END

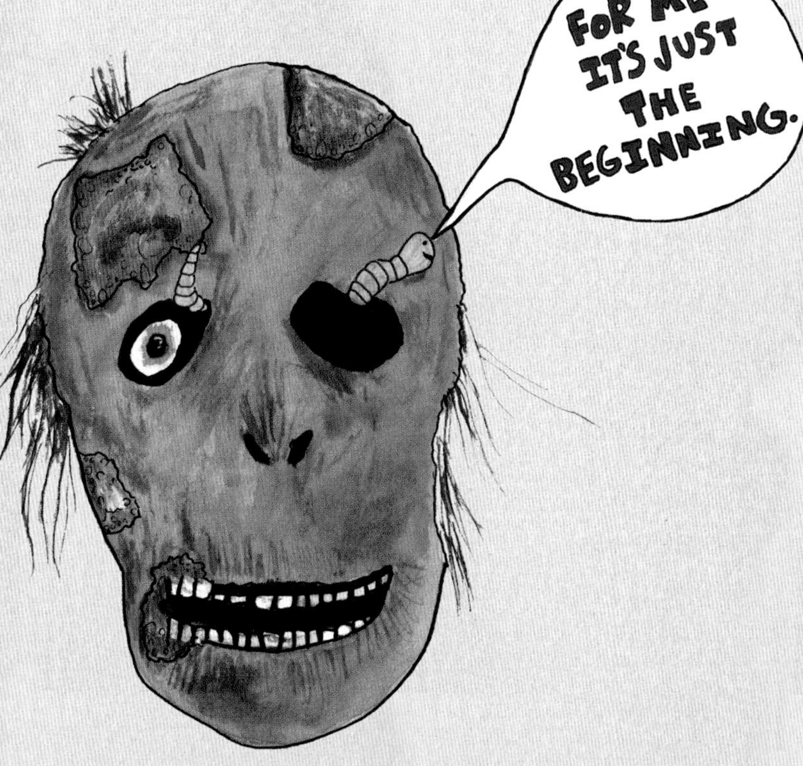
FOR ME IT'S JUST THE BEGINNING.

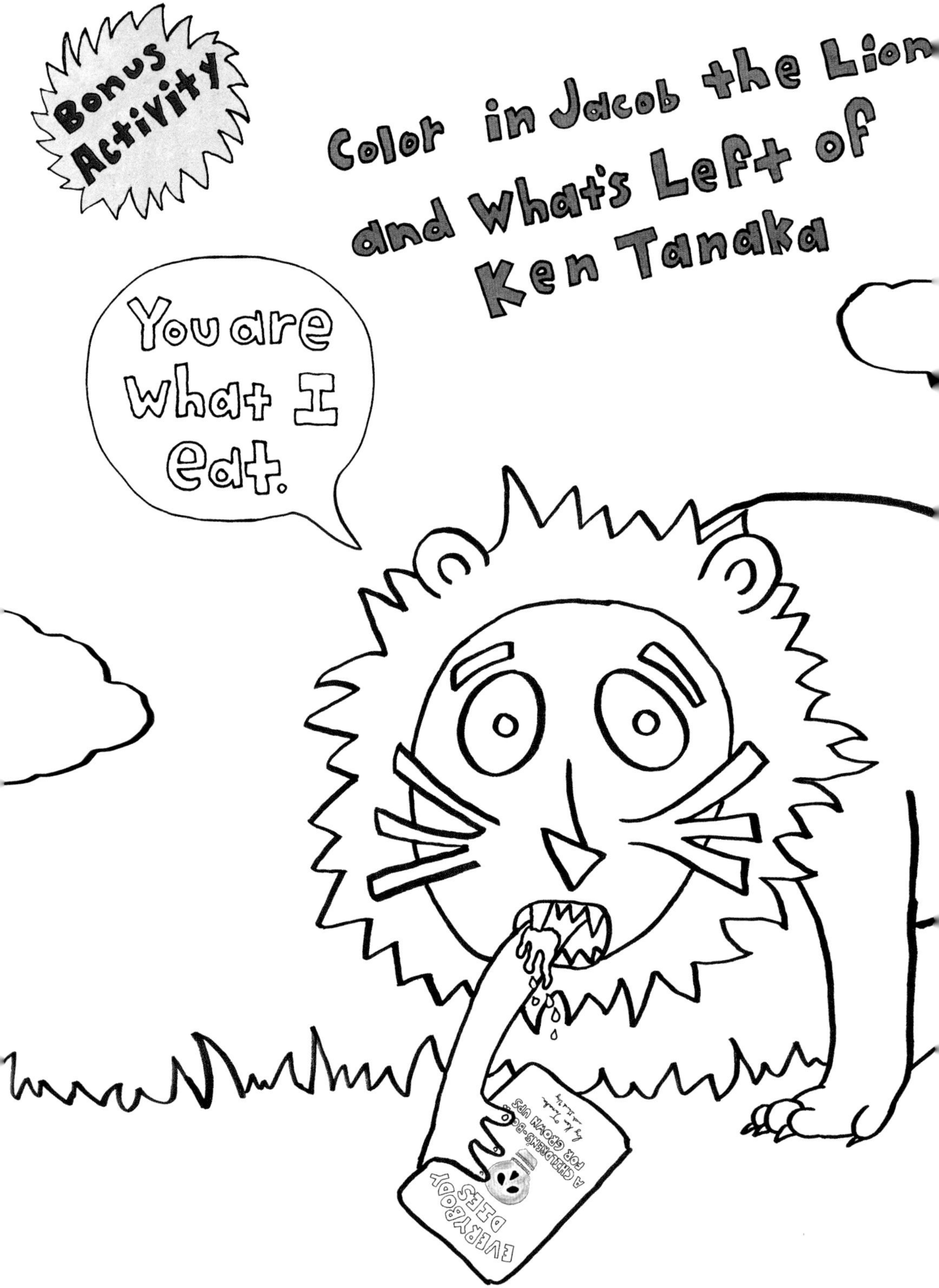

Bonus Activity
Color in Jacob the Lion and What's Left of Ken Tanaka
You are what I eat.
EVERYBODY DIES
A CHILDREN'S
FOR GROWN UPS

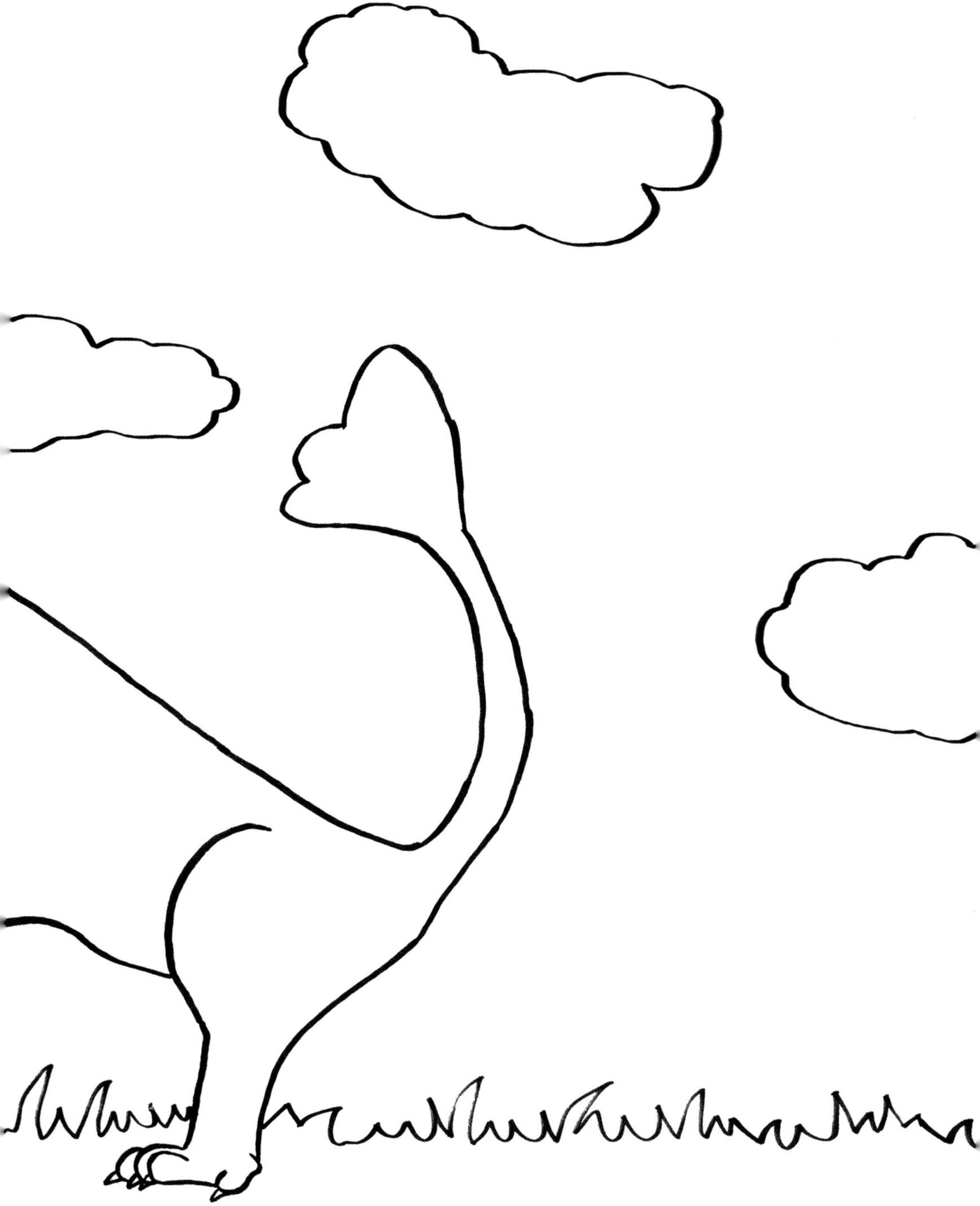

KEN TANAKA PICTURE BOOKS

COLLECT THEM ALL*

POLAR BEAR, POLAR BEAR, WHAT THE F**K?
GHOSTS ARE REAL AND THEY'RE AFTER YOU
Ken Tanaka's Big Book of Parasites
IA. ROUNDWORM
A CHILDREN'S GUIDE TO HEAVY ARTILLERY

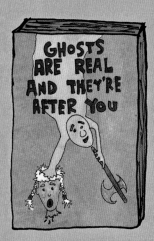

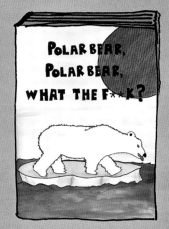

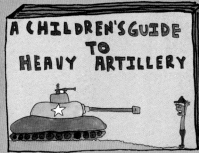

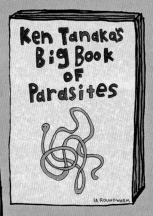

*(Books do not actually exist)

KEN
TANAKA
LOVES
YOU.

Self-Portrait of Me As Someone Else

Ken Tanaka

Born in Los Angeles as Ken Smith, Ken Tanaka was adopted by a Japanese family and raised in rural Shimane Prefecture. At the age of thirty-three, Ken returned to Los Angeles to search for his birth parents with only their names, Jonathan and Linda Smith. He documented his search on YouTube and quickly became an online sensation. His award-winning videos include the viral hit "What Kind of Asian Are You?", the White Samurai series, and "What Is Art?" In late 2007 Ken was reunited with his long-lost twin brother and "Everybody Dies" coanchor, David Ury, via YouTube (search Ken Tanaka meets David Ury on YouTube). The two of them have been collaborating ever since. When Ken is not busy with his search for the Smiths, he spends his time painting funny people and animals. In 2009 the famed Los Angeles gallery Billy Shire Fine Arts held his now-historic inaugural art show, "Maximum Pleasant," a humorous blend of Japanese and American pop culture. You can visit his art and animal friends at WWW.KenTanakaLovesYou.Com.

David Ury

Author, actor, and stand-up comic David Ury has
a long history with death. While he is best known
for getting crushed by an ATM as the character Spooge
in AMC's "Breaking Bad", he has been shot, bitten,
impaled, and stabbed to death countless times in
American films and television programs. David's
first acting role was in a high school production of
"Riders to the Sea." He played the role of Bartley, an Irish
fisherman who spent most of the play lying dead onstage,
which made his mother cry. He has written nearly
one hundred English language adaptations of foreign
comics including "Me and the Devil Blues", which won a
Glyph Award in 2009. You can find his work at
WWW.DavidUry.Com.

Thank You

This book would not have been possible without the support of the following very handsome friends and animals.

Mari, Hideo and Junpei Tanaka, Jonathan and Linda Smith, Leah and Naomi, James Jean, Karen and Carl, Frank and Debra, Gary Musgrave, Signe Bergstrom, Keith Knight, Lonnie Millsap, Jacob the happy rabbit, Todd Moyer, Cam Floyd, SKU, Stella Choe, Naomi Grossman, Ray Katsuyuki, Dolly, Paul, and Carrie, David Mack, Josh Glaser, Billy Shire, Lucas Gray, Lebasse Projects, Mari Araki, Julia Abramoff, Deanne Oi, Takeo-Kun, Polo-Kun, Jerry Leibowtz, Jordan Feldman, Ria Fay-Berquist, Matt Murdock, Annie Adjchavanich, Remi February Kitsune Suzuki, YouTube, Ginmeabreakman, Hikosaemon, You (The one reading this right now) Everyone at D.H. and Armada, Jordan Smith, Miles Beller

And our Sponsor

Daizen brand Mineral Water

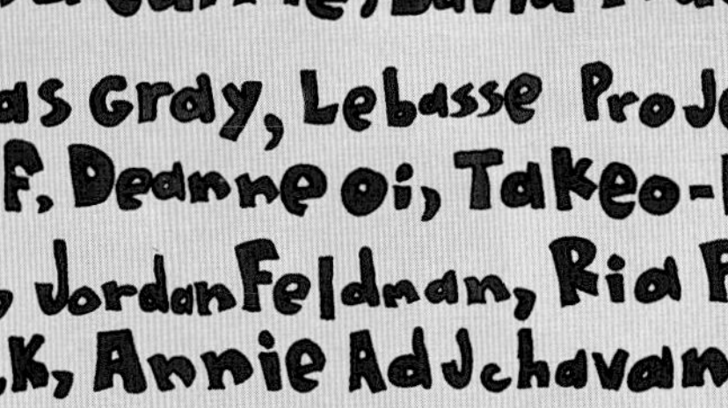

TANAKA
大山

The Wettest Water in the World

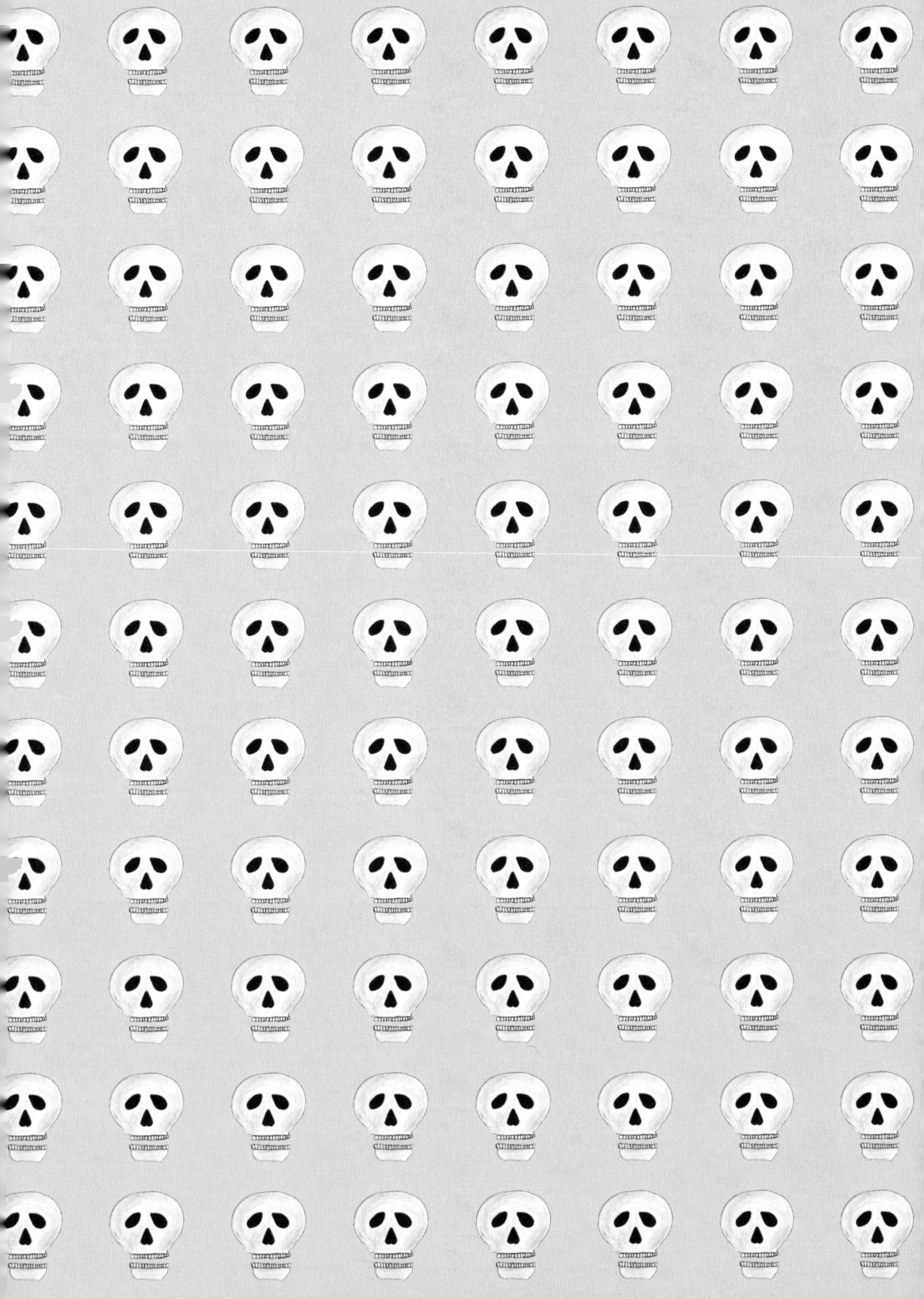

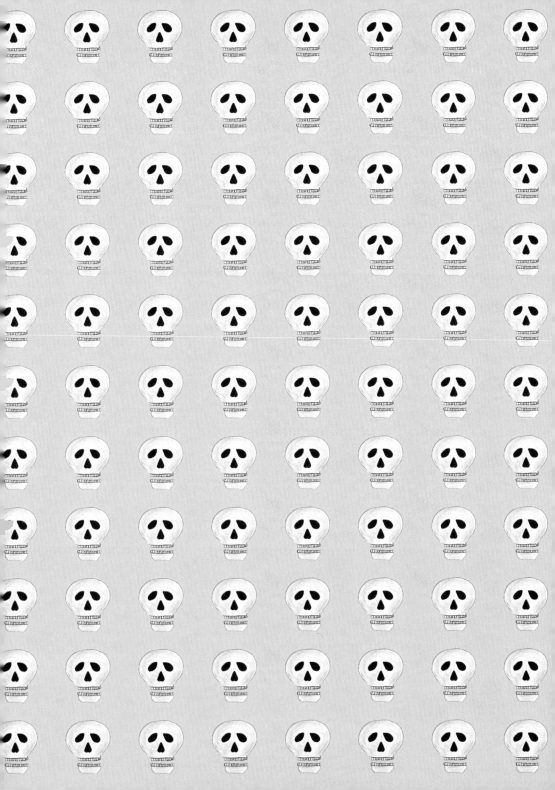

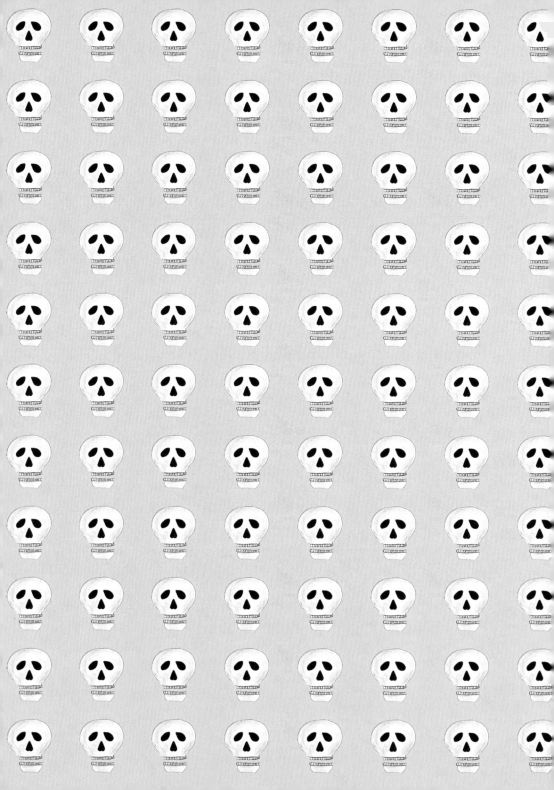